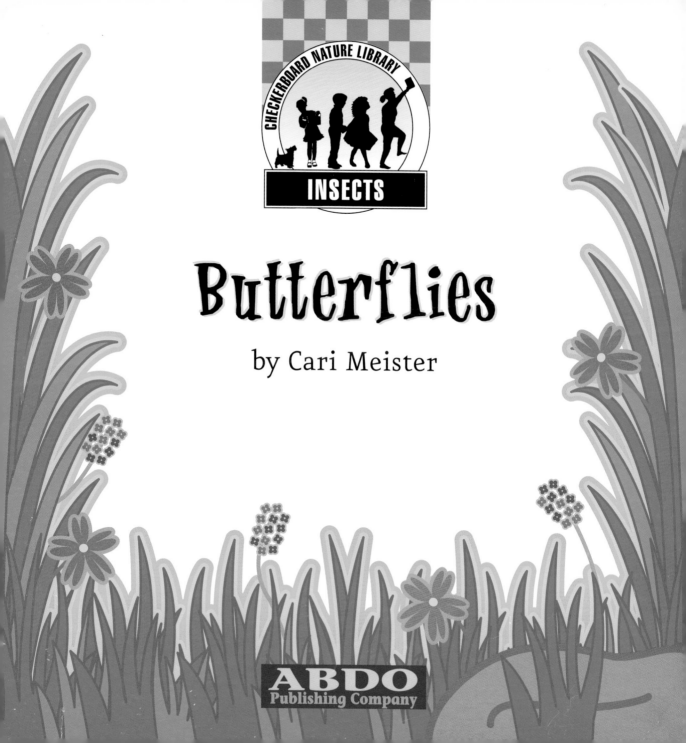

Butterflies

by Cari Meister

visit us at
www.abdopub.com

Published by ABDO Publishing Company, 4940 Viking Drive, Suite 622, Edina, Minnesota 55435. Copyright © 2001 Abdo Consulting Group, Inc., Pentagon Tower, P.O. Box 36036, Minneapolis, Minnesota 55435 USA. International copyrights reserved in all countries. No part of this book may be reproduced in any form without written permission from the publisher.

Printed in the United States

Illustrators: Edwin Beylerian, Carey Molter

Cover photo: Eyewire Images

Interior photos: Artville, Corbis Images, Digital Stock, Digital Vision, Eyewire Images, Peter Arnold, Inc., PhotoDisc

Editors: Tamara L. Britton, Kate A. Furlong

Design and production: MacLean & Tuminelly

Library of Congress Cataloging-in-Publication Data

Meister, Cari.
    Butterflies / Cari Meister.
       p. cm. -- (Insects)
    ISBN 1-57765-459-5
    1. Butterflies--Juvenile literature. [1. Butterflies.] I. Title.

QL544.2 .M44 2000
595.78'9--dc21

00-056881

Contents

What is a Butterfly? 4

The Butterfly's Body 6

How They Grow 10

What They Eat..12

Where They Live 14

Enemies...16

Butterflies & People 18

Fun Facts 20

Glossary 22

Web Sites 23

Index 24

What is a Butterfly?

Butterflies are amazing insects. There are more than 100,000 kinds of butterflies in the world! They live on every **continent**. Butterflies come in many colors, patterns, and sizes. Some butterflies are big and spotted. Some butterflies are little and solid.

During its life, the butterfly goes through many changes. It starts out as a small, hungry caterpillar. Then it becomes a **chrysalis**, which spends much time growing. Finally, it is ready to enter the world as a beautiful butterfly!

Butterflies are fun to watch. But they are also important to the **environment**.

Young butterfly caterpillars eat many plants and leaves. When adult butterflies eat, they **pollinate** many plants.

Butterflies pollinate many plants.

The Butterfly's Body

A butterfly's body has three main sections. These sections are the head, thorax, and abdomen. The head is the front section of a butterfly's body. The thorax is the middle section. The abdomen is the last section. Each section is made up of smaller parts. All of these parts make up an adult butterfly.

A butterfly's head has two **antennae**. The antennae are long and slender. They have a sense of smell, which helps the butterfly find **nectar**. Antennae also warn butterflies of dangerous animals. Male butterflies use their antennae to find female butterflies.

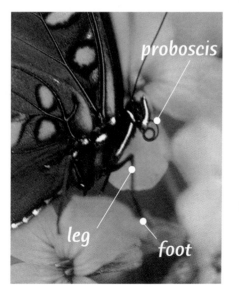

proboscis

leg

foot

A butterfly's head also has eyes. Butterflies have compound eyes. Compound eyes are made up of many smaller eyes called facets. Facets sense movement and color.

antenna

eye

head

thorax

abdomen

Besides eyes and **antennae**, a butterfly's head also has a **proboscis**. A butterfly uses its proboscis to eat. It works like a straw, which allows the butterfly to suck **nectar** easily. When a butterfly is not eating, its proboscis coils up like a snake.

A butterfly's wings are attached to the thorax. The wings are made up of many **veins**. The veins make a butterfly's wings strong. The wings are covered with tiny scales. Each scale has a color. These colored scales overlap like the shingles on a roof. This creates beautiful patterns on the butterfly's wings.

Just like its wings, a butterfly's legs are attached to the thorax. Every butterfly has six strong legs. Butterflies use their legs to hold onto flowers as they eat. The feet on the butterfly's front legs are special. They have the butterfly's taste buds.

A butterfly's abdomen has many organs in it. The abdomen holds a butterfly's heart. The heart pumps blood. The abdomen also holds the gut. It digests food. Organs used for mating are also found in the abdomen.

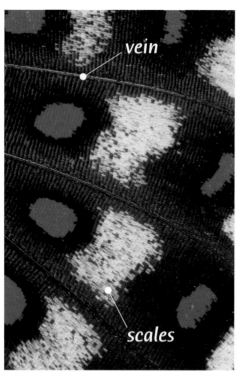

A close-up view of a butterfly wing.

Butterflies do not have bones to protect their organs. Instead, they have exoskeletons. An exoskeleton is a hard casing on the outside of an insect's body. It helps protect the inside organs from being smashed or crushed.

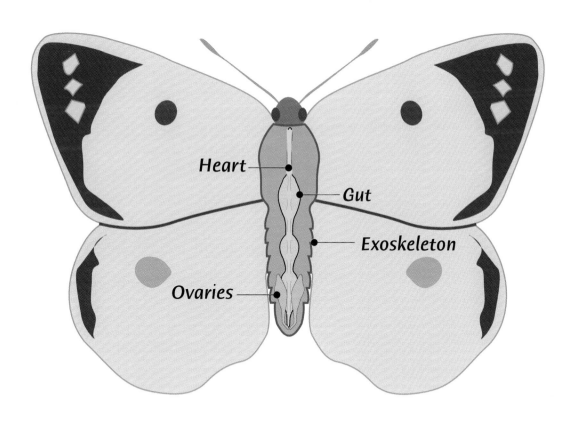

Heart

Gut

Exoskeleton

Ovaries

How They Grow

As a butterfly grows, it goes through many changes. These changes are broken into four stages. The stages are called egg, larva, pupa, and adult.

Every butterfly begins life as an egg. Each female butterfly can lay between 50 and 1,000 eggs. Most butterflies lay their eggs on leaves. Each kind of butterfly has different eggs. Some eggs are round and some are oval. Though most eggs are smooth, a few have ridges.

When the eggs hatch, butterfly larvae crawl out. Butterfly larvae are called caterpillars. A caterpillar spends its time eating. It grows quickly. As it grows, the caterpillar's skin becomes too small. So, it sheds its skin often.

When the caterpillar is fully grown, it stops eating. It grabs hold of a stem with its hind legs. Then the caterpillar's skin splits. It sheds its old skin. The new skin forms a hard shell around the caterpillar. During this time, the caterpillar becomes a pupa. A butterfly pupa is called a chrysalis. Amazing changes happen to the chrysalis. It begins to change into an adult butterfly.

After several weeks, an adult butterfly breaks from the shell. Its wings are wet and weak. It waits for them to dry and harden. Then it can fly away to look for food.

adult butterfly

pupa

larva (caterpillar)

eggs

What They Eat

As soon as a caterpillar breaks from his egg, it starts eating. In fact, the caterpillar's first meal is often its eggshell. Caterpillars are very hungry creatures. They eat lots of leaves. They have strong mouthparts to rip and tear leaves apart.

Some kinds of caterpillars, like the monarch caterpillar, eat poisonous plants. The plants do not harm the caterpillars. The plants only hurt the animals that try to eat the caterpillars.

A tent caterpillar eats a pear leaf.

When caterpillars turn into butterflies, they stop eating leaves. Adult butterflies eat flower **nectar**. This gives butterflies energy and makes them strong. It also **pollinates** many plants. Some butterflies do not eat nectar. They feed on tree sap. Or, they drink the juices from rotten fruits.

A Cethosia hypsea, also called a malay lacewing, feeds on a flower.

Where They Live

Butterflies live all over the world. They live in many different climates. Some butterflies live in cold mountain regions. A small white butterfly, called Butler's Mountain White, lives in the Himalayan mountains. Its dirty white coloring helps it blend into the mountains.

Bright colored butterflies live in hot, tropical areas. Birdwing Swallowtails are bright green. They live in New Guinea. Cattle Heart Swallowtails have spots of red and green. They are found in Central and South America.

The Dead Leaf butterfly blends in with its surroundings.

There are more kinds of butterflies in mixed woodlands than anywhere else on Earth. A mixed woodland is a place with many kinds of trees and plants. Mixed woodlands are found in **temperate** regions. Many butterflies that live there are brown. They may be hard to spot. They blend right into the trees and dirt!

Brown butterflies often live in woodland areas.

Enemies

Butterflies have many enemies. Birds, insects, spiders, and lizards like to eat butterflies. Some insects, such as the stinkbug, feed on butterfly eggs. Other insects, such as the praying mantis, feed on caterpillars.

Caterpillars have several ways to protect themselves from enemies. Some caterpillars have prickly spikes. Many caterpillars can blend into their environment. For example, a green caterpillar sometimes looks like part of the leaf it's eating!

Butterflies can also blend into their environment. The Indian Leaf butterfly can disappear right into the ground. Its brown underside looks exactly like decaying leaves!

The stinkbug and praying mantis are two of the butterfly's enemies.

16

A butterfly's wings also protect it from enemies. Some butterfly wings have eyespots. They look like tiny eyes. Eyespots scare away enemies. Some butterfly wings have bright colors to warn enemies that they are poisonous. Other butterflies **mimic** the way the poisonous butterflies look. That way, enemies will stay away from them even though they are not poisonous. This is called mimicry.

Some butterflies and caterpillars have eyespots that scare enemies away.

Butterflies & People

In some societies, butterflies are important symbols. Butterflies stand for change. They also stand for natural beauty. Some people collect butterflies.

Most people like to see butterflies. They are colorful. They have pretty patterns. They **flit** through the sky. They do not bite or sting. Many people do not like to see caterpillars. Caterpillars can be pests. They eat a lot. Sometimes they eat so much they destroy crops.

Butterfly morpho.

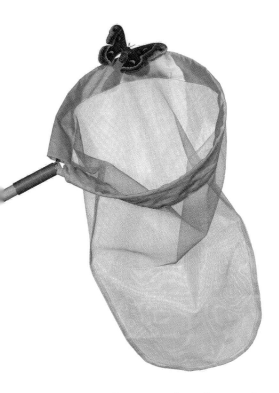

Many people collect and display butterflies.

Today, butterflies are in danger. In many parts of the world, people are clearing away areas where butterflies live. People are building homes and offices, where there used to be woods. Without the proper plants to eat, butterflies die. Many species are nearly **extinct**. It is up to people to save them.

Fun Facts

🦋 The word *butterfly* comes from the yellow-colored Brimstone butterfly that arrives in Europe in early spring. People used to call it the "butter-colored fly" because it was yellow. Over time the name was shortened to "butterfly."

Brimstone butterfly.

🦋 Butterflies are closely related to moths. One way to tell them apart, is by watching what time of the day they are active. Most butterflies are active during the day. Most moths are active at night.

Some butterflies, like the Monarch butterfly, **migrate** to escape cold weather.

Monarch butterfly.

You can attract butterflies to your yard. Different kinds of plants attract different kinds of butterflies. Milkweed and thistle are two common butterfly-attracting plants.

Eastern black swallowtail on a thistle flower.

Index

body, 6, 7, 8, 9, 16, 17

caterpillars, 4, 5, 10, 12, 13, 16, 18

chrysalis, 4, 10

colors, 4, 8, 14, 16, 17, 18

development, 4, 10, 11

enemies, 16, 17

food, 5, 6, 7, 8, 11, 12, 13, 19

home (habitat), 14, 16, 19

kinds, 4, 14, 15, 16

patterns, 4, 8, 14, 15, 18

people, 18, 19